404556R00015

Made in the USA
Middletown, DE
08 October 2023

# My 1ST

# HOCKEY BABY BOOK

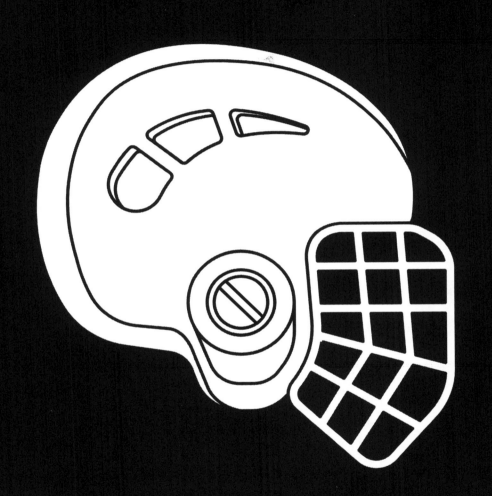

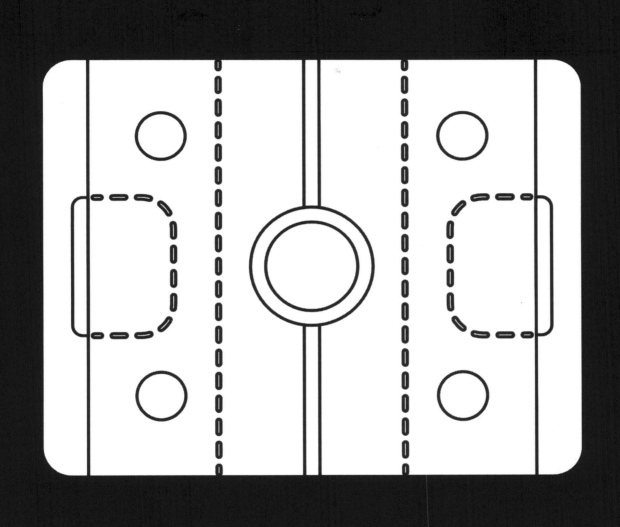

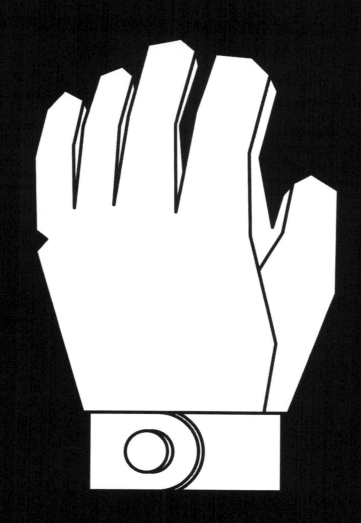

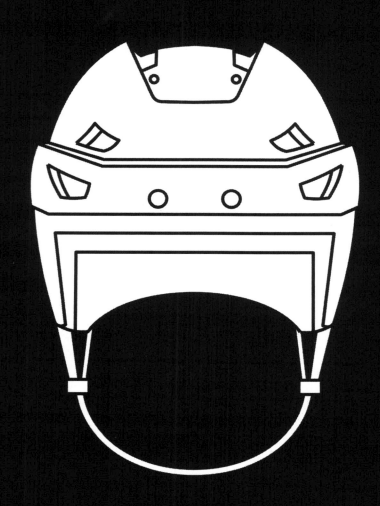

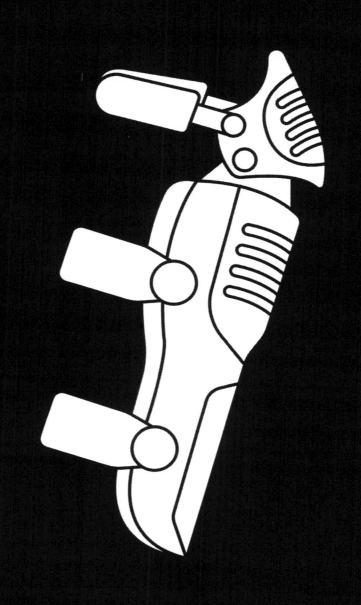

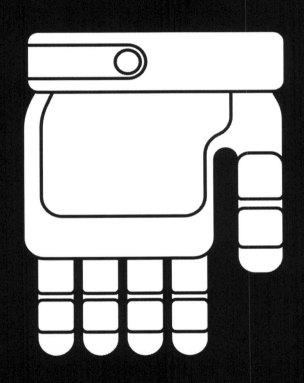

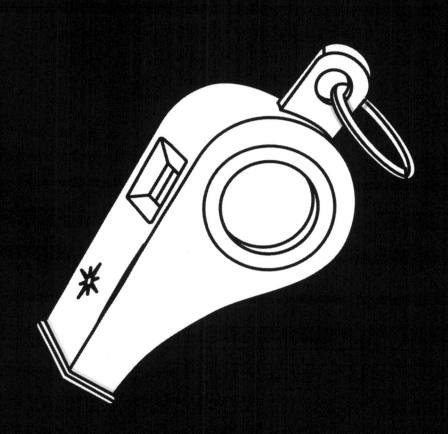

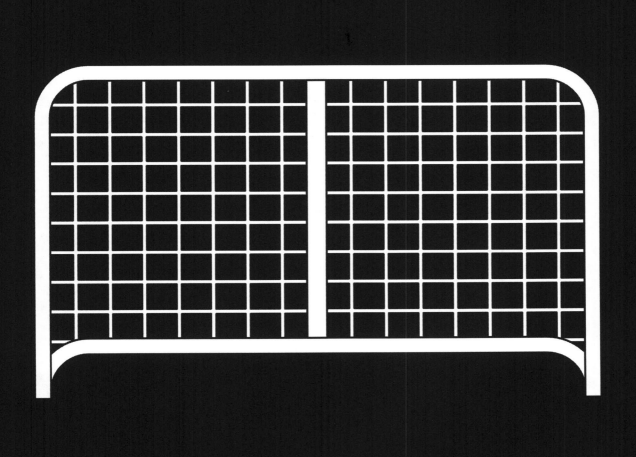

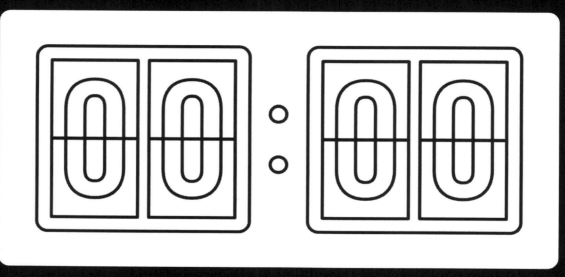

Thank you for getting my book!

If you find this hockey baby book fun and useful.
I would be very grateful if you posted a review on Amazon!
Thanks to your review. I can improve myself and it will help me
create better books.

If you would like to leave a review.
just head on over to this book's Amazon page and click
"Write a customer review".

Thank you. your support matters!

I invite you to visit my author's page
where you can find other interesting products.

## Abbigail Lillie Publishing